The Refugee Camp

by Jim Eldridge

illustrated by Tom Sperling

CAMBRIDGE
UNIVERSITY PRESS

Institute of Education

Chapter 1

'Ahmed! Ahmed!'

Eleven-year-old Ahmed cut infield, heading for the Tent City goal. The supporters of Jaystars chanted and shouted in excitement.

Jaystars were one of the best teams in the refugee camp's Under-15 Football League.

The rest of the Tent City team ran back as fast as they could to protect their goal. The Tent City central defender, Bozan, a tall powerfully-built boy of almost fifteen, was the only one between Ahmed and the goalkeeper.

A roar went up from Jaystars' supporters as Ahmed flicked the ball past Bozan.

'Shoot!' yelled the crowd, excitedly.

CRUNCH!!

Boos and shouts of disapproval were heard as Bozan made a crunching tackle from behind, that caught Ahmed's ankle and sent him crashing to the hard, dusty sand.

Ahmed rolled over, his face wreathed in pain.

The referee blew his whistle and wagged a warning finger at Bozan.

Ahmed's best pal, Mustafa, helped Ahmed to his feet.

'That hurt!' winced Ahmed.

He looked at his ankle, which was bruised and bleeding from the studs of Bozan's boot.

'The referee should have sent Bozan off,' complained Mustafa. 'That was a goal-scoring opportunity. If you'd have scored, we'd have drawn. And with Tent City, the top team in the league!'

'Maybe Urdal will score from the free kick,' said Ahmed.

'No chance!' said Mustafa. 'Tent City have had time to get their defence back in place.'

Mustafa was right. Urdal's shot was blocked by the wall of defenders. As the ball was kicked into touch, the final whistle went, with Tent City the winners, 3-2.

As Ahmed limped off the pitch, he found Bozan blocking his path. And not just Bozan. Bozan's gang was with him, and it included some older boys.

'How's your ankle?' sneered Bozan, nastily.

Ahmed didn't answer. Bozan and his gang had a bad reputation as bullies in the camp.

Bozan put his face close to Ahmed's.

'You made me look a fool today!' he said, angrily. 'You made me look slow!'

'I was just playing football!' protested Ahmed.

'If you ever do that to me again, what I did to your ankle will be just the start!' Bozan said, threateningly.

Then he stamped on Ahmed's injured foot and pushed him so hard that Ahmed fell to the ground.

'Remember what I said!' sneered Bozan.

Mustafa had seen what happened, and came over to Ahmed after Bozan and his gang had gone.

'Are you alright?' asked Mustafa.

'Yes,' said Ahmed, getting to his feet. 'He's just a bully.'

'He's a bully with a gang, and he's bigger and tougher than you,' said Mustafa. 'He's really angry that you scored twice against his team today. No one's done that to him before. That's why Tent City are the top of the League. If you take my advice, you'll keep away from him.'

'At least we won't be playing Tent City again for a while,' said Ahmed.

Chapter 2

Ahmed limped back to the tent where he lived with his mother and young sister, Jamila. His ankle still hurt, but he would bathe it and put leaves on it. That usually helped to heal any injuries.

The refugee camp was an enormous tented city where many thousands lived. Like everyone else living there, Ahmed had escaped from a war zone. He and his mother and sister had fled across the border to this camp from their own country, after the city they lived in was bombed. Ahmed's father had died in the bombing.

Everyone in this tented city was waiting: either for the war to end so they could go home; or to get to another country and start a new life. Ahmed wanted to go to Europe. He had seen magazines with photographs of the great cities in Europe, and as a football fan, his big ambition was to play for one of the top European clubs.

A football charity organised the Junior Football League in the camp, where teams of boys under fifteen played against one another. Ahmed's team, Jaystars, was in the top half of the League. That was good, considering that the boys were just eleven and twelve years old. Most of the boys in the other teams were thirteen or fourteen.

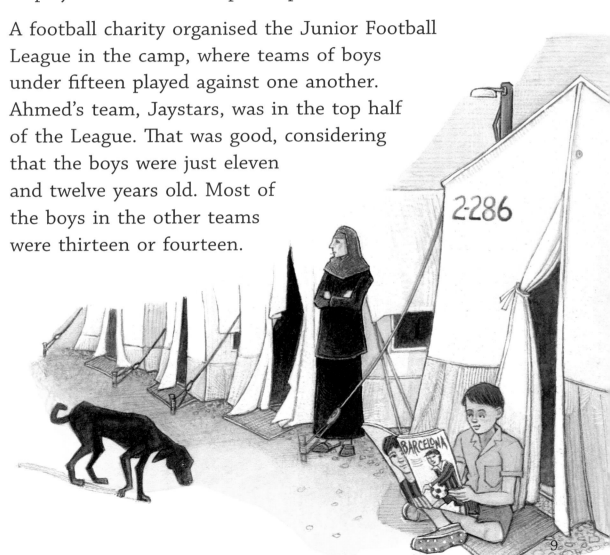

Because Ahmed played as a forward, he was often the target for hard tackles. Bozan's tackle today had been the nastiest. Bozan was the worst kind of bully. And he got away with things because he was big and tough, and he had a gang.

It was a few days before Ahmed saw Bozan again. Ahmed had gone with his mother and Jamila, to collect their rations from the latest charity delivery. Bozan and his gang were also there, picking up their families' rations. Ahmed helped his mother and Jamila carry the flour and oil to their tent, and then went back to collect their rice. As he was walking away from the collection point, he turned a corner down one of the tented streets and came face to face with the gang.

'Look who it is!' sneered Bozan. 'The boy who made me look a fool in front of everyone.'

Bozan strode to Ahmed and took hold of his bag of rice.

'Well you can pay me back for what you did. I'm taking that rice!'

'No!' shouted Ahmed, and he held on tightly to the bag of rice.

'Waz! Maki! Hold his arms!' Bozan shouted at his gang.

The two big boys headed towards Ahmed, who held the bag of rice even tighter.

'No!' shouted Ahmed again. 'This is ours!'

'What's going on here?' demanded an angry voice.

The bullies turned and looked at the man who'd just appeared. He was old and leaning on a stick. He glared at Bozan and the gang.

'I can't believe it!' he shouted. 'You're stealing rice from another family!'

At this, the boys in Bozan's gang looked uncomfortable and stepped away from Ahmed. Bozan let go of the bag of rice.

'We are all refugees here!' stormed the man, angrily. 'We have escaped from the people who persecute us! And yet you persecute this boy and try to steal his rice? You should be ashamed of yourselves! We must all work together. That is the only way we will survive this. People like you are bad for this camp. I will report you to the camp authorities. What are your names?'

The boys exchanged scared looks. They all looked at Bozan, worried expressions on their faces. Bozan looked frightened and hung his head, avoiding the old man's angry glare.

'You're too scared to give your names. Is that how brave you are?' the man shouted. 'Well, I shall find out who you are. Especially you!' And he pointed an accusing finger at Bozan.

Some women had gathered at this commotion, and now they also pointed accusing fingers at the bullies and made noises of disapproval.

The old man turned to Ahmed. 'Who are these boys? You must know their names.'

Ahmed looked at the gang. They looked back at him, pleading looks on their faces as they begged him not to say.

'I don't know them,' said Ahmed.

The man looked questioningly at Ahmed. Then he turned back to Bozan and the gang.

'I shall be watching you!' he warned them, angrily.

The murmurs of discontent from the watching women grew louder, and Ahmed was shocked to see that Bozan had burst into tears. Then he ran off, covering his face with his hands. His gang followed him.

The old man turned to Ahmed.

'You'd better get to your family with that rice. If those boys come after you, shout and I'll come.'

'Thank you,' said Ahmed.

'I'm not sure I did the right thing,' thought Ahmed. 'Bozan will hate me even more because I saw him crying. He's going to have his revenge on me for sure because of that.'

'I hate my life here,' he thought angrily, as he hurried back to his family's tent.

Then, he calmed down. 'No, I don't really hate it here. Here, we're safe from the bombing and killing that went before.' But Ahmed remembered the time before that: the time of being happy, when he and his family lived in a big house in a lovely part of their city. His father had been a surgeon at the hospital, loved and respected by everyone. Ahmed and Jamila had gone to good schools with great teachers. Their mother enjoyed her work at a clinic. It had been a perfect life.

And then the war came. Bombs raining down on the city, whole streets destroyed. Ahmed's father had been working at the hospital, carrying out an operation, when it had been hit. He'd been killed, along with other doctors and nurses, and patients.

Then their house had been hit, as were many others.
Lots of their neighbours had been killed.

'We will die if we stay here,' said his mother.

So they'd packed some essential things and joined the hundreds of people fleeing the city and heading for the nearest border.

And here they were, with their previous life just a memory. Just waiting. But for how long?

Chapter 3

After the incident with the rice, Ahmed did his best to keep away from Bozan. If he saw Bozan walking down one of the streets, he went by another route to avoid him. Once, he was horrified to see Bozan actually hanging around outside his family's tent. Ahmed's mother also saw him and went out to ask what he wanted, but Bozan said nothing, and just walked away.

Ahmed told his friends, Mustafa and Mezut, about what had happened over the rice, and the old man coming to his rescue. But he didn't tell them about Bozan crying. It didn't seem right to tell them.

'At least you won't have to see Bozan any time soon,' said Mezut. 'We haven't got another game for a couple of weeks, and that's against Sandy City, and they're younger than us.'

But, as it turned out, Ahmed would be seeing Bozan a lot sooner than expected.

There was great excitement in the camp. It had been announced that there was going to be a surprise visit by a team of young professional footballers, the International Junior All-Stars, and they were going to play a match against a team chosen from the under-15 League teams.

'They're bound to choose you, Ahmed,' Mezut and Mustafa told him. 'You're one of the top scorers in the League.'

'I hope they do,' thought Ahmed. The idea of appearing on the same pitch as these young professionals filled him with excitement. But when the notice was put up with the names of the team, Ahmed's wasn't there. All the players selected were those who were fourteen. And the team included Bozan.

'Well, I don't care about Bozan,' Ahmed told himself determinedly. 'Because he's playing, I'm bound to see him, but there's nothing that will stop me going to the game.'

On the day of the match, Ahmed made his way to the camp football pitch. Unlike the football stadiums that Ahmed had seen on television, this was just the same as any local football pitch: a roped-off area with a goal at each end, with the crowd standing behind the ropes to watch. Because it was in the desert, the playing surface was rough and dry. Ahmed followed the crowd. It seemed as if everyone in the camp was heading towards the game. When he got near the pitch, Ahmed's heart sank as he saw Bozan and his gang. Ahmed had hoped that Bozan would be practising with the team, or that he'd meet Mustafa and the others before he ran into them.

Ahmed was just about to turn back and try a different street, when Bozan shouted at him: 'Ahmed! I've been looking for you!'

Before he could get away, Ahmed found himself surrounded by Bozan's gang.

'I'm going to have to fight them,' he thought miserably. 'But there are too many of them!'

Bozan stepped forward and, to Ahmed's surprise, said: 'I've been looking for you to say sorry for the way we tried to take your rice. What the old man said was right. We're all refugees. We should help one another. I was angry because you made me look a fool in front of everyone, but now I know you didn't mean to. You're just a better footballer than me.

You could have given that man our names and got us all in trouble. But you didn't. We owe you for that.' He held out his hand. 'Will you shake my hand, as a friend?'

Stunned, Ahmed took Bozan's hand and shook it. Then, one by one, the rest of the gang shook Ahmed's hand.

'Right,' said Bozan. 'I have to go and get ready for the match.' To his gang, he said: 'Make sure that Ahmed gets a good place at the front of the crowd.'

Chapter 4

The match was the best ever seen at the camp. The camp team played with lots of passion and energy, but the professionals from the International Junior All-Stars team were far more skillful. Soon, the score was 1-0 to them, and not long after, 2-0.

Then the camp team were awarded a penalty for a handball, and their striker made it 2-1. This gave them more heart, and the game seemed to become even faster.

In the second half, it was obvious that the camp team were getting tired, while the young professionals of the International All-Stars seemed just as fit and energetic, and they launched a fierce attack on the camp team goal. Their centre forward ran at speed towards the goal, the ball at his feet, and was lining up to fire a shot when Bozan hurled himself in front of the striker and deflected the ball into touch for a throw-in.

Bozan went to get up from where he'd fallen, then collapsed, clutching his thigh in pain.

The coach came running onto the pitch.

'What's happened?' he asked.

'It's my hamstring!' groaned Bozan.

The coach looked serious.

'We haven't got anyone as good as you to substitute,' he said.

'Yes you have,' said Bozan. 'Put on Ahmed from Jaystars in my place. He's a great footballer.'

'But he's only eleven. And he's not a defender.'

'Trust me, if you put him on, you won't need another defender,' said Bozan. 'He'll keep the All-Stars tied up in front of their goal.'

'Come on,' urged the referee. 'You have to get your player off the pitch. We've got to keep the game going.'

The coach nodded. While two players helped Bozan off, the coach ran to where Ahmed was standing.

'Get some boots on, Ahmed,' he said. 'You're playing.'

Ahmed stared at him, shocked.

'Me?'

'Yes,' nodded the coach. 'Bozan said you're the best, and I trust him.'

'But ... my boots are in my tent,' said Ahmed. 'I have to get them.'

'There's no time for that,' said the coach. 'There are only four minutes left.'

'Try my boots,' said Bozan.

Quickly, Ahmed put on the boots. Yes, they fitted!

The camp team had defended strongly while they were down to ten. As Ahmed ran onto the pitch, the ball bounced towards him. He trapped it and then began to run down the touchline, faster than he'd ever run before. He went past one player, then another. He looked up to see who in his team was near the All Stars' goal, but no one was there: they had all been defending their own goal, and Ahmed's run upfield had caught them by surprise. He was on his own.

Ahmed changed direction, heading infield, leaving another All-Stars player struggling behind him. The All-Stars central defender advanced on Ahmed, and then went in for a hard tackle on the smaller player. But, just as he had done before, against Bozan, Ahmed leapt into the air, over the defender's outstretched leg, nimbly dodging the tackle, and collected the ball again. A swerve and Ahmed was past the other central defender. The All-Stars goalkeeper advanced towards Ahmed, crouching low, arms stretched wide on either side.

Flick!

It was the cheekiest of chips over the goalkeeper's head, too high for him to get a hand to. The ball dropped down and bounced over the line into the goal.

The equaliser – 2-2!

The crowd went wild, cheering and shouting, and leaping up and down. The noise of the celebrations was so loud that the referee had to blow harder than usual to make his whistle heard to signal the end of the game.

As Ahmed came off the pitch, he was mobbed by his friends from the Jaystars, and everyone else. Bozan limped to Ahmed and hugged him.

'I knew you could do it!' he said.

Ahmed felt a hand on his shoulder. He turned and looked into the smiling face of the All-Stars manager.

'That was a brilliant goal you scored,' said the manager. 'If I can get you a trial for a professional team, would you be interested?'

'Yes!' burst out Ahmed.

'I'll see what I can do,' said the manager. 'I think you've got a great future.'

The All-Stars manager went back to his own players.

'You've done it, Ahmed!' shouted Mustafa, excitedly. 'You're going to be famous!'

Ahmed smiled to himself. This could be the first step towards his dream.

'It's not about the fame,' he told himself. 'I just want a new life for my mother and my sister.

A better life.'

The Refugee Camp *Jim Eldridge*

Teaching notes written by Sue Bodman and Glen Franklin

Using this book

Content/theme/subject

Ahmed's dream is to play professionally for a European football team – it is his hope for a better life for himself and his family. This story of triumph over adversity offers opportunity to explore different points of view. The challenging themes emerging (bullying, effects of war) have capacity for emotional engagement and in-depth reaction.

Language structure

- Emotive language (*'I hate my life here'* p.16) describes character feeling.
- Grammatical conventions support the action and character responses, such as short sentences for impact.

Book structure/visual features

- Events occur over time and in flashback.
- Chapters support the build-up and suspense of the narrative.

Vocabulary and comprehension

- Word choices challenge comprehension, such as in the use of adverbs to support characterisation (*'determinedly'*, on p.21) and specialist language (*'penalty'*, *'deflected'*, *'striker'* on p.24).
- The writer evokes a response in the reader, for example when Bozan breaks down in tears (p.15).

Curriculum links

Geography – Children could investigate their favourite teams, mapping the countries of origin of the players.

PSHE – Use Ahmed's experiences and real-life news items to explore sensitively the plight of refugee children in different parts of the world.

Learning outcomes

Children can:

- explain their views to others and listen to points of view which may differ from their own
- recognise narrative structure techniques (such as flashbacks) and consider their effectiveness
- identify ways in which grammatical conventions and language structures support reading comprehension.

Planning for guided reading

Lesson One Explaining and justifying viewpoint

Introduce the book, discussing what the children know already of refugees and why Ahmed might be in the camp. Read the background to Ahmed's story on pp.17-18. Turn to pp.2-3 and discuss what has happened. Establish the two teams and the characters of Bozan and Ahmed.

Set an independent reading task to read Chapter 1. Listen in and support comprehension, for example in clarifying unfamiliar vocabulary, such as *'winced'* on p.3, and Mustafa's use of conditional verbs on p.4.

Bring the group together and discuss the threat Bozan made to Ahmed (p.6). Point out how the author positions the reader by his choice of vocabulary, for example on p.5: *'… sneered Bozan, nastily.'*

Follow up after the lesson: Children reread Chapter 1 and read Chapter 2 in preparation for the next lesson.

Lesson Two Narrative structure techniques

Begin the lesson by reviewing the story so far.